2005 2006 Greatest Pop Hits

This book is part of an instrumental series arranged for Flute, Clarinet, Alto Sax, Tenor Sax, Trumpet, and Trombone. The arrangements are completely compatible with each other and can be played together or as solos. Each book contains a carefully edited part that is appropriate for the Level 2-3 player.

A Violin book is also available as a part of this series. The arrangements in the Violin book, however, are not compatible with those in the wind instrument books due to level considerations regarding keys and instrument ranges.

Contents

BEAUTIFUL

Words and Music by
JIM BRICKMAN, JACK KUGELL
and JAMIE JONES

Slow ballad (♩ = 60)

Verse:

Chorus:

rit.

25317

4

BECAUSE OF YOU

4Words and Music by
KELLY CLARKSON, BEN MOODY
and DAVID HODGES

Moderately slow (♩ = 72)

4Because of You - 2 - 1
25317

4© 2004 Smelly Songs, SmellsLikeMetal Publishing and Dwight Frye Music, Inc.
All Rights for SmellsLikeMetal Publishing Administered by Dwight Frye Music, Inc. (BMI)
All Rights Reserved

Chorus:

mp

BELIEVER

Words and Music by
will.i.am and John Legend

EMOTIONAL

Words and Music by
ANDREAS CARLSSON,
DESMOND CHILD and CHRIS BRAIDE

BOULEVARD OF BROKEN DREAMS

Words by BILLIE JOE
Music by GREEN DAY

Boulevard of Broken Dreams - 2 - 1
25317

Verse 3:

D.S. 𝄋 al Coda

Coda

rit.

BREAKAWAY

Words and Music by
MATTHEW GERRARD, AVRIL LAVIGNE
and BRIDGET BENENATE

Moderately slow (♩. = 52)

Verse:

Chorus:

EVERYTHING BURNS

Words and Music by
BEN MOODY

Moderately slow (♩ = 96)

Verse 1:

Chorus:

Everything Burns - 2 - 2
25317

GOOD IS GOOD

Words and Music by
SHERYL CROW and JEFF TROTT

I'M FEELING YOU

Words and Music by
JOHN SHANKS,
MICHELLE BRANCH
and KARA DIOGUARDI

HUNG UP

Words and Music by
MADONNA, STUART PRICE,
BENNY ANDERSSON and BJÖRN ULVAEUS

Moderate dance beat (♩ = 120)

INSIDE YOUR HEAVEN

Words and Music by
ANDREAS CARLSSON, PER NYLEN
and SAVAN KOTECHA

Slowly (♩ = 69)

Inside Your Heaven - 2 - 1
25317

LIKE WE NEVER LOVED AT ALL

Words and Music by
JOHN RICH, VICKY McGEHEE
and SCOTT SACKS

LOST WITHOUT YOU

Words and Music by
MATTHEW GERRARD and
BRIDGET BENENATE

Slowly (♩ = 72)

Verse:

Chorus:

To Coda

1. *2.* *Bridge:*

D.S. al Coda

Coda

25317

MAGIC WORKS

By JARVIS COCKER

NO MORE CLOUDY DAYS

Words and Music by
GLENN FREY

STICKWITU

Words and Music by
FRANNE GOLDE, KASIA LIVINGSTON
and ROBERT PALMER

Slowly (♩ = 72)

Verse:

mf

% *Chorus:*

To Coda ⊕

1. 2. *Bridge:*

D.S. % al Coda ⊕ *Coda*

rit. e dim.

OVER

Words and Music by
JOHN SHANKS, KARA DIOGUARDI
and LINDSAY LOHAN

Moderately slow (♩ = 88)

Verse:

Chorus:

To Coda ⊕

1.

Over - 2 - 1
25317

PHOTOGRAPH

Lyrics by CHAD KROEGER
Music by NICKELBACK

Slowly (♩ = 76)

Verse:

mf

(Play cue note 2nd time)

𝄉 *Chorus:*

Photograph - 2 - 1
25317

READY TO FLY

Words and Music by
RICHARD MARX

STRANGER IN A STRANGE LAND

Words and Music by
BARRY GIBB, ASHLEY GIBB
and STEPHEN GIBB

UNTITLED
(How Can This Happen to Me?)

Words and Music by
SIMPLE PLAN

Moderately slow (♩ = 92)

Untitled - 2 - 1
25317

WAKE ME UP WHEN SEPTEMBER ENDS

Words by BILLIE JOE
Music by GREEN DAY

WHEN YOU TELL ME THAT YOU LOVE ME

Words and Music by
ALBERT HAMMOND and JOHN BETTIS

Slowly (♩ = 76)　　*Verse 1:*

Verses 2 & 3:

Chorus:

When You Tell Me That You Love Me - 2 - 1
25317

WINDOW TO MY HEART

Words and Music by
JON SECADA and
MIGUEL MOREJON

Moderate dance tempo (♩ = 104)

Bridge:

a tempo

Chorus:

rit.

YOU AND ME

Words and Music by
JUDE COLE and JASON WADE

You and Me - 2 - 1
25317

PARTS OF A FLUTE AND FINGERING CHART

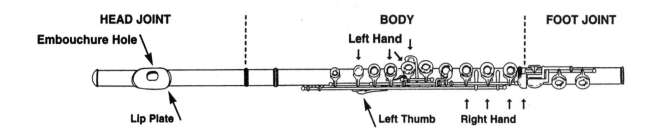

● = press the key.
○ = do not press the key.

When there are two fingerings given for a note, use the first one unless the alternate fingering is suggested.

When two enharmonic notes are given together (F♯ and G♭ as an example), they sound the same pitch and played the same way.